6.6

No Lex 2114

PEACHTREE CITY
PLAN TO STAY™

PEACHTREE CITY LIBRARY
201 Willowbend Road
Peachtree City, GA 30269-1623
Phone: 770-631-2520
Fax: 770-631-2522

YOUR FAMILY TREE

Collecting Primary Records

by Jim Ollhoff

Visit us at
www.abdopublishing.com

Published by ABDO Publishing Company, 8000 West 78th Street, Suite 310, Edina, MN 55439. Copyright ©2011 by Abdo Consulting Group, Inc. International copyrights reserved in all countries. No part of this book may be reproduced in any form without written permission from the publisher. ABDO & Daughters™ is a trademark and logo of ABDO Publishing Company.

Printed in the United States of America, North Mankato, Minnesota
052010
092010

 PRINTED ON RECYCLED PAPER

Editor: John Hamilton
Graphic Design: Sue Hamilton
Cover Design: John Hamilton
Cover Photo: iStockphoto
Interior Photos: Ancestry.com-pgs 15 & 19; AP-pgs 9 & 17; Corbis-pg 7; Getty Images-pg 11; Granger Collection-pgs 12, 13 & 21; iStockphoto-pgs 1, 3, 5 & 29; Library of Congress-pgs 4, 7, 14, 18 & 27; RavenFire Media-pgs 6, 16, 20, 25, 26 & 28; Story County Iowa Atlas and Plat Book-pg 24; Thinkstock-pgs 8, 10, 22 & 23.

Library of Congress Cataloging-in-Publication Data

Ollhoff, Jim, 1959-
 Collecting primary records / Jim Ollhoff.
  p. cm. -- (Your family tree)
 Includes index.
 ISBN 978-1-61613-461-7
 1. Genealogy--Juvenile literature. I. Title.
 CS15.5.O44 2010
 929'.1072--dc22
                    2009050811

Contents

The Importance of Primary Records

One thing every serious genealogist does is collect primary records. These are also called primary sources, or primary documents. A primary record is something created by an eyewitness to an event, someone who was there when the event happened. It can be an official document, like a birth certificate, or it can simply be a journal or letter written by an eyewitness. The sooner the document is created after the event, the better.

Below: A New York birth certificate from 1913. This official document is a primary record.

Primary documents are important because they are the most reliable information about your ancestors. They identify when your ancestors came to this country, when they got married, when they were born, and when they died. If you don't have primary documents, then all you have are rumors and hearsay.

Above: A letter or journal entry may be a primary document.

A secondary record is something that is created later, by somebody else, sometimes long after an event occurs. Secondary records are usually (but not always) less reliable than primary records. Hazy memories, exaggeration, and inaccurate transcribing can affect the accuracy of secondary records.

A death certificate, for example, records both the birth date and the death date of a person. It is a primary document for the death date, because it is filled out shortly after a person dies. However, it is a secondary source for the birth date. That's because the doctor or person filling out the death certificate would often simply ask family members for the information. Grief-stricken relatives may give the correct birth date, but perhaps not.

Of course, there are problems in searching for and finding primary documents. In times past, before fire alarms and smoke detectors were common, fire was a constant danger. Fire has destroyed many courthouses where primary documents were kept. Other records may be difficult to read because of water damage or improper storage. Sometimes the people who wrote the documents had poor penmanship, and today we can't decipher what they wrote. Sometimes the documents were filled out incorrectly.

Still, primary documents are the best way we have to look backward in time. These documents can help us pinpoint important events in the lives of our ancestors. This book identifies the most common primary and secondary documents, what they can tell us, and where to find them.

Above: A fire in the United States capitol building in Washington, D.C., damaged the House Document Room in January 1930.

Above: Firefighters in London, England, battle a blaze caused by German bombing of the city during World War II.

Birth and Death Certificates

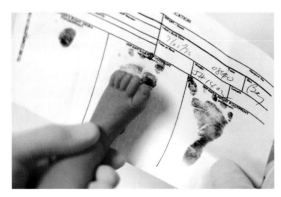

Above: When a person is born today, the hospital or doctor creates a birth certificate.

When a person is born today, the hospital or doctor creates a birth certificate. When a person dies, the county government usually creates a death certificate. These documents record important information in addition to birth and death dates, including addresses, cause of death, parents' names, and spouses.

These documents are available from the county where the birth or death occurred. They are usually stored in the county's department of vital records. It is often possible to get photocopies of these documents for a very small fee. Check with the department of vital records in the county where your ancestors were born or died. Usually, a Google search that includes the name of the county, plus "vital records," will send you to the right place.

Most states started requiring birth and death certificates in the early 1900s. Many counties required certificates earlier than that. You'll have to find out when certificates began to be created in the state and county that you're researching.

Above: Books containing Ohio birth certificates are stored in the Ohio Department of Health Vital Statistics building. Counties across the United States all have similar storage of birth certificates for all the people born in their area. Some of the birth certificates date back more than 100 years.

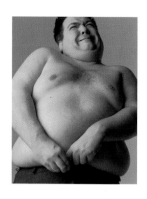

Above: An old death certificate might list "pants too tight" as the cause of death.

On death certificates, one of the blanks that is filled in is the "cause of death." You should regard this information suspiciously, especially on death certificates that are very old. In previous generations, medical science was not fully developed. Many older death certificates use terms that modern medicine no longer uses. However, even some of the more bizarre causes of death can give us clues. For example, if you scout through death certificates from the early 1900s, you might come across a cause of death listed as "pants too tight." While this is humorous at first, it pays to look deeper. In the late 1800s and early 1900s, doctors were not yet familiar with viruses. In those days, influenza (the "flu") was often fatal, and doctors didn't understand that viruses were the cause. Desperate to identify the cause of the terrible sickness, doctors guessed about all kinds of possible causes. Some doctors actually thought that people got influenza when their pants were too tight.

It is helpful to get copies of your ancestors' siblings' certificates, too. It is estimated that about 20 percent of birth and death certificates have errors on them. So, while you're asking for your great-great grandfather's birth certificate, ask for the certificates of his brothers or sisters, too, if they're available. You'll be able to crosscheck the certificates to make sure all names, dates, and addresses match.

Above: Surgery being conducted in 1880. Doctors were not familiar with viruses and germs, and often couldn't identify what caused a person's death.

Immigration and Naturalization Records

If your family came here from another country, there are three kinds of records you should search for: passenger lists, immigration records, and naturalization papers.

Passenger lists are primary records that list people who were passengers on a ship. The captain would write down a list of everyone on the ship who was entering the United States. Many of these lists are now preserved in books. Other lists are available online, or in archived records in the port of entry.

Immigration records, or "certificates of arrival," were taken at the city of entry into the United States. Clerks would list the people who were entering the country. Many countries also have *emigration* records, which list the people who were departing to live in another country. Unfortunately, many of those records, especially in Europe, have been destroyed by war or fire.

Below: An Italian family arrives at Ellis Island, New York, in 1905.

Above: A ship of immigrants arrives in New York Harbor in 1905.

Naturalization papers are the government documents that officially mark when a person becomes a citizen of the United States. On a document called an *Intent to Naturalize*, people renounce allegiance to their former country and declare their intent to become a United States citizen. Usually, you can find the country of their birth on this document. Finally, the actual naturalization papers, called a *Certificate of Naturalization*, formally made the immigrant a citizen. The Certificate of Naturalization was usually given out several years after the Intent to Naturalize document. The Intent to Naturalize document was no longer required after 1952.

Keep in mind that up to 25 percent of immigration in the 1800s and early 1900s was illegal. Many people snuck into the United States to live. For other people, their paperwork was lost or accidentally destroyed.

Many naturalization and immigration records are available online. Sometimes a fee is required.

Below: Immigrants attend a naturalization class in the 1920s. The class was given to prepare people to become citizens of the United States.

Above: The ship *Umbria* and a few pages of its 15-page passenger list. The ship traveled in March 1887 from Liverpool, England, to the port in New York City.

News Clippings and Obituaries

Prominent City Doctor Dies

DR. A. W. POLICOFF

Death, as it must to all men, came to Dr. Arthur William Policoff, one of this city's best known practitioners and heart experts, yesterday morning in the Royal Victoria Hospital, Montreal. The doctor had been suffering ever since his return from a special post-graduate course at Ann Arbor, Michigan.

He leaves to mourn a wife, Sarah, a seven year old daughter, Barbara Ann and a brother William in Montreal. The late doctor's father predeceased him a year ago.

Dr. Policoff, who later rose in the heart of the capital's people to one of its most popular doctors, came here in 1932 for a year's internship at the General Hospital after graduation in medicine at McGill University.

Following internship, Dr. Policoff entered private practice and in face of many difficulties, gradually built up his practice until it grew to one of the largest in the city. Quiet and gentlemanly in demeanour he made many friends here who greatly regret his early passing.

When death came, he was in his 41st year.

Above: Obituaries can provide interesting facts about people.

Newspaper articles and obituaries can be rich sources of information about your ancestors. An obituary is a notice printed after a person dies. It is a secondary source, but it often gives useful, personal facts about the deceased person. It commonly identifies the cause of death and the surviving family. Sometimes it gives much more information—hobbies, interests, and involvement in the community.

Some obituaries are online. Most obituaries are buried in newspaper microfilm. Microfilm are pictures that are taken of each page of the newspaper and then reduced to a tiny size. Your best bet is to find the newspaper in the area where your ancestor lived, and then find out if the newspaper has archives. If they do, find out how to access them. Usually, you'll have to go to the newspaper building, or possibly the local public library. There, you'll have to find the right microfilm and put it into a microfilm reader. A librarian can usually help you. It can be time-consuming, but if you find your ancestor, it's worth the time and trouble.

Not all your ancestors will have an obituary. But it's worth a look to see if it's out there.

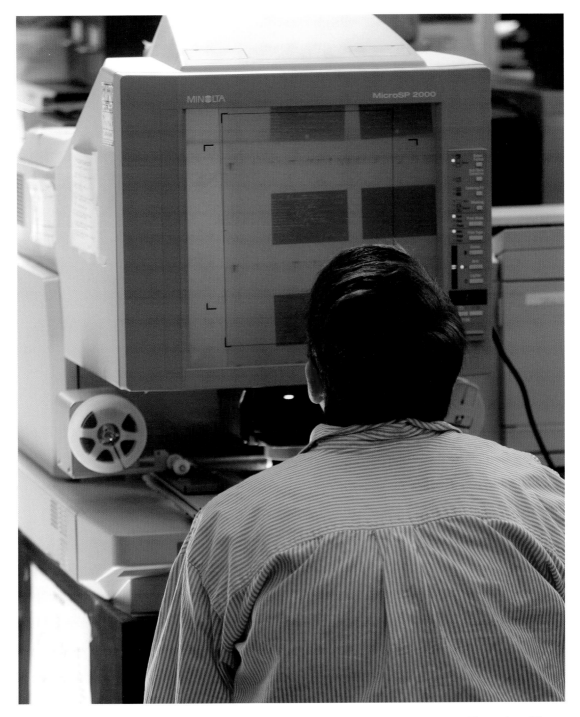

Above: Microfilms at the Bennington Museum in Bennington, Vermont. The microfilm contains records of every birth, marriage, and death recorded by Vermont's town clerks from 1908 to 1941.

The Census

Searching through the United States census is a very common and important way to find out information about your ancestors. It is a unique mix of primary and secondary information, sometimes full of facts you might not find anywhere else.

The first United States census happened in 1790. Every 10 years since then, another census has been taken. The federal government produces the census. Today, the United States Census Bureau mails questionnaires to nearly every household in the country. The bureau also hires workers to visit households that don't respond to the questionnaire.

The kind of information collected by the census has changed over the years. Early in the history of this country, census takers only identified the "head of the household." Beginning in 1850, the census identified every person who lived in the household. The information taken in each census varies a little bit. You can usually find people's names and ages, the address of the house, immigration information, and other kinds of information. It can be a treasure-trove of knowledge about your family.

Above: A page from the 1790 census, taken in the town of Lynn, Massachusetts.

U.S. DEPARTMENT OF COMMERCE
Economics and Statistics Administration
U.S. CENSUS BUREAU

United States Census 2010

This is the official form for all the people at this address. It is quick and easy, and your answers are protected by law.

Use a blue or black pen.

Start here

The Census must count every person living in the United States on April 1, 2010.

Before you answer Question 1, count the people living in this house, apartment, or mobile home using our guidelines.

- Count all people, including babies, who live and sleep here most of the time.

The Census Bureau also conducts counts in institutions and other places, so:

- Do not count anyone living away either at college or in the Armed Forces.
- Do not count anyone in a nursing home, jail, prison, detention facility, etc., on April 1, 2010.
- Leave these people off your form, even if they will return to live here after they leave college, the nursing home, the military, jail, etc. Otherwise, they may be counted twice.

The Census must also include people without a permanent place to stay, so:

- If someone who has no permanent place to stay is staying here on April 1, 2010, count that person. Otherwise, he or she may be missed in the census.

1. How many people were living or staying in this house, apartment, or mobile home on April 1, 2010?

   Number of people =

2. Were there any additional people staying here April 1, 2010 that you did not include in Question 1? Mark X all that apply.
   - Children, such as newborn babies or foster children
   - Relatives, such as adult children, cousins, or in-laws
   - Nonrelatives, such as roommates or live-in baby sitters
   - People staying here temporarily
   - No additional people

3. Is this house, apartment, or mobile home — Mark X ONE box.
   - Owned by you or someone in this household with a mortgage or loan? Include home equity loans.
   - Owned by you or someone in this household free and clear (without a mortgage or loan)?
   - Rented?
   - Occupied without payment of rent?

4. What is your telephone number? We may call if we don't understand an answer.
   Area Code + Number

OMB No. 0607-0919-C: Approval Expires 12/31/2011.
Form D-1 (12-5-2008)
USCENSUSBUREAU

5. Please provide information for each person living here. Start with a person living here who owns or rents this house, apartment, or mobile home. If the owner or renter lives somewhere else, start with any adult living here. This will be Person 1.
   What is Person 1's name? Print name below.
   Last Name
   MI
   First Name

6. What is Person 1's sex? Mark X ONE box.
   - Male
   - Female

7. What is Person 1's age and what is Person 1's date of birth? Please report babies as age 0 when the child is less than 1 year old. Print numbers in boxes.
   Age on April 1, 2010   Month   Day   Year of birth

→ NOTE: Please answer BOTH Question 8 about Hispanic origin and Question 9 about race. For this census, Hispanic origins are not races.

8. Is Person 1 of Hispanic, Latino, or Spanish origin?
   - No, not of Hispanic, Latino, or Spanish origin
   - Yes, Mexican, Mexican Am., Chicano
   - Yes, Puerto Rican
   - Yes, Cuban
   - Yes, another Hispanic, Latino, or Spanish origin — Print origin, for example, Argentinean, Colombian, Dominican, Nicaraguan, Salvadoran, Spaniard, and so on.

9. What is Person 1's race? Mark X one or more boxes.
   - White
   - Black, African Am., or Negro
   - American Indian or Alaska Native — Print name of enrolled or principal tribe.

   - Asian Indian
   - Chinese
   - Filipino
   - Other Asian — Print race, for example, Hmong, Laotian, Thai, Pakistani, Cambodian, and so on.
   - Japanese
   - Korean
   - Vietnamese
   - Native Hawaiian
   - Guamanian or Chamorro
   - Samoan
   - Other Pacific Islander — Print race, for example, Fijian, Tongan, and so on.
   - Some other race — Print race.

10. Does Person 1 sometimes live or stay somewhere else? Mark X all that apply.
    - No
    - Yes
      - In college housing
      - In the military
      - At a seasonal or second residence
      - For child custody
      - In jail or prison
      - In a nursing home
      - For another reason

→ If more people were counted in Question 1, continue with Person 2.

Right: The 2010 census. To protect people's privacy, information from this census will not be released to the public until 2082, 72 years later.

Census statistics are readily available, but to protect people's privacy, personal information is not released to the public for 72 years. Some census data is available online. If you want to search for free, many public libraries have census data. But you won't find anything from the 1890 federal census. Most of the 1890 census information was lost in a fire in 1921.

The federal government isn't the only organization that has conducted censuses. Most states have conducted censuses also. Check online or with your library to find out if and when your state's censuses were taken.

Above: An 1854 painting by Francis William Edmonds of a census taker.

Like everything else in genealogy, census information should be taken with a grain of salt. Sometimes the information is incorrect. Sometimes people fudge their ages a bit, to make themselves look older or younger than they really are. Some people give the wrong marriage date to hide the fact that they had children before they were married. In the past, sometimes people spoke in a language that the census taker didn't understand, so the worker wrote down what he *thought* they said. Sometimes the handwriting of the census taker was illegible. Also, some census takers may not have completed their job properly.

Still, despite all the problems, most of the census data is correct, and it will provide generous amounts of information about your family. It is a vital step in searching for your family members. Once you find your ancestors in the census, you know where they lived. Next, you can search for more records at the county level.

Cemeteries

Walking through a cemetery can be a very peaceful experience. Finding your ancestors in a cemetery can be a somber but wonderful discovery. Many people like to take pictures of the headstones of their ancestors.

The death date on a gravestone is usually reliable information. The birth date is sometimes wrong. The headstone carver has to rely on a grieving relative to remember the date. Looking near your ancestor's gravestone will sometimes give information, too. Are there relatives buried nearby? How about parents or children?

Below: Over time, rain, moss, and age can make headstones barely readable.

Over time, rain, moss, and age take their toll on headstones. Sometimes they are barely readable. Sometimes you'll need a spray bottle of water and a soft cloth to clear the moss from the headstone. If your ancestor has a gravestone that is unreadable, you may be able to do a grave rubbing. Place a piece of paper or newsprint over the headstone, and then use a crayon to rub across the paper. This will leave darker marks where the indented words are. With a grave rubbing, it is sometimes possible to decipher an unreadable gravestone.

Above: Finding your ancestors in a cemetery can be a wonderful discovery.

Other Records to Search

Below: A 1926 plat map from Story County, Iowa.

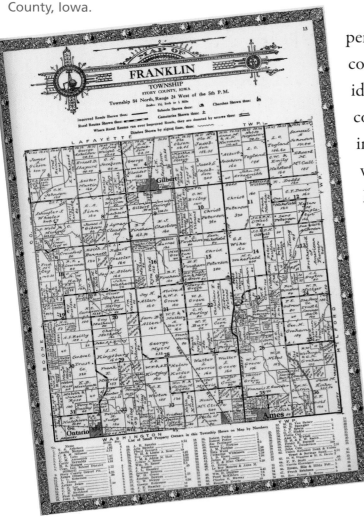

There are many other primary and secondary records for you to search.

Plat maps were periodically created by counties. These maps identified who owned county land. These can be invaluable to find exactly where your ancestors lived. Most counties keep records of land sales, too. These documents are located in the county offices, often in the office of vital records. Tax records will show how much money people paid in taxes. This information might help you determine where an ancestor lived, and how much land they owned.

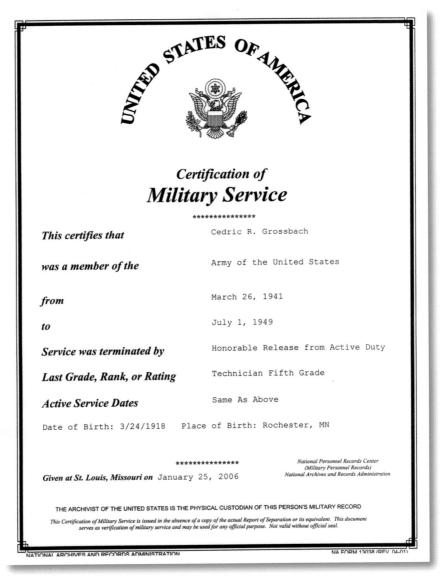

Above: A certificate showing military service. Records such as this one may be ordered by relatives from the federal government's National Archives.

If your ancestor served in the military, you might be able to access their military records. Their records may show their years of service, their awards, and sometimes even the battles they fought. It might be possible for you to order these records from the federal government's National Archives. Unfortunately, a fire in 1973 destroyed 16–18 million military personnel files.

Marriage Certificate

STATE OF MINNESOTA
COUNTY OF **Olmsted**

I hereby certify, that on **August 21** , 19 **81** , at **Rochester, Minnesota** , in said County,
I, the undersigned, a **United Methodist minister** did join in marriage:

John Charles Hamilton of the County of **Olmsted** State of **Minnesota** , and
Sue Louise Grossbach of the County of **Olmsted** State of **Minnesota**
The names of the parties after their marriage, shall be: **John Charles Hamilton** , and
Sue Louise Hamilton

In the presence of:

Jim Oellhoff
(Signature of Witness)
(Type or Print Name)

Dee Malcomson
(Signature of Witness)
(Type or Print Name)

R C Painter
(Signature of Officiating Person)
(Type or Print Name) **R. C. Painter**

2645 North Broadway
(P.O. ADDRESS)

Rochester, Minn. 55901

Credentials Recorded: **LeSueur** County, Minn.

(One duplicate certificate to be given to each of the parties married.)

K3111 OSWALD PUBLISHING CO., NEW ULM, MINN.

Above: A marriage certificate from 1981. Marriage certificates began to be required in the late 1800s and early 1900s.

Marriage certificates began to be required in the late 1800s and early 1900s. Check the county's office of vital records to find marriage certificates. Usually, but not always, marriages were performed in the county where the wife's family lived.

Church records are another important source of information about ancestors. Churches typically kept records of baptisms, marriages, and deaths. You might be able to get a baptism certificate or other kinds of official documents.

Some counties have published histories of their own counties. Sometimes there are biographies of prominent citizens in these books. Maybe you'll be lucky and find an ancestor there! These books are available in county libraries and history centers. Some counties and towns also produced city directories. These listed individuals and their occupations.

There are different kinds of death records besides medical records. If the person had a Social Security number, Social Security death records will identify their date of death. Getting this information usually requires an online subscription to a genealogy service. Your local library might be a subscriber, which means you can research for free if you have a library card. Ask a librarian for help.

Probates and wills can identify how the possessions and home of a deceased person were distributed to surviving family members. These documents are typically found in county records offices, or at county historical societies.

Finally, some of the best kinds of primary documents are letters, diaries, and correspondence of your ancestors. These can be wonderful, rich windows into the lives your ancestors lived.

Below: A diary page written by Admiral George Dewey of the United States Navy. The entry is from May 1910. Diaries, letters, and other correspondence can give vital information into the type of life your ancestors lived.

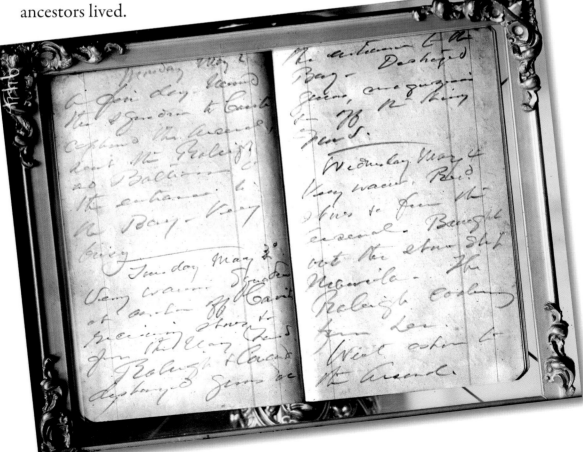

What's Next?

Above: An example of an acid-free album in which old documents can be safely stored.

When you get an old primary document, you'll want to preserve it as long as possible. Some papers have acids in them that will degrade the documents over time. You can minimize that problem by storing them in acid-free plastic folders. All old documents should be stored in acid-free plastic if you want to keep them for a long time. You might want to make copies of old documents to use in your daily research. File the originals away for safekeeping.

Once you have collected primary and secondary documents, another step might be to study what it was like during the time your ancestors lived. What else was going on in the world at that time? When did your ancestors come to this country? What might be some reasons they left their old country? Studying daily life of another time is called social history. It might give some insights into why your ancestors started a new life in a new country.

Another possibility is to look at your DNA. You can't see your own DNA, of course. But there are companies that can analyze your DNA to see if you are related to another group of people. The DNA tests can even look back through time—tens of thousands of years—to see where your ancient ancestors came from.

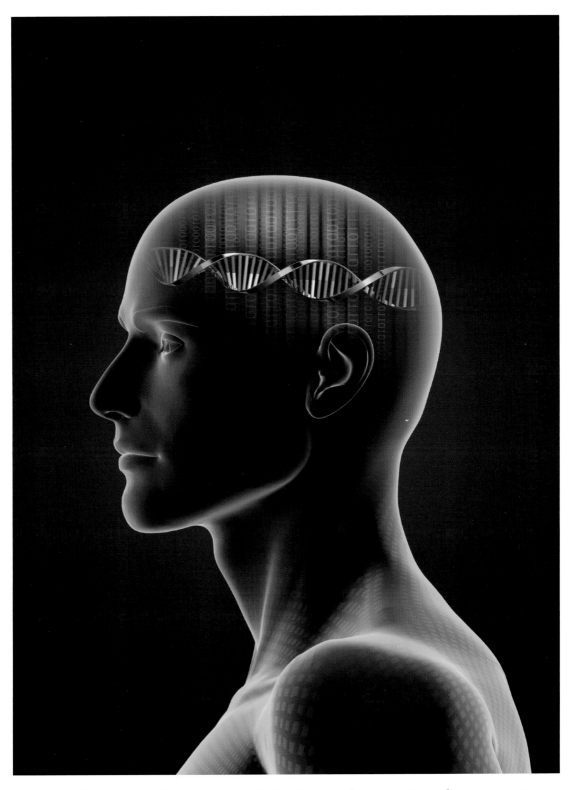

Above: A DNA test may help you look at the history of immigration of your ancestors.

Glossary

ACID-FREE

A paper or plastic that minimizes the normal degrading of very old documents.

ANCESTORS

The people from whom you are directly descended. Usually this refers to people in generations prior to your grandparents.

EMIGRATION

The process of leaving one country to live in another. For example, *Jacob O'Malley emigrated from Ireland.*

FEDERAL CENSUS

The federal government's records that show information about who lives in this country and where. Also, the process of collecting that information.

GENEALOGY

The study of your ancestors and your family history.

IMMIGRATION

The process of entering a country in order to live there. For example, *Jacob O'Malley immigrated to the United States.*

OBITUARY

A printed report of a person's death.

PLAT MAP

A map that identifies who owns land in a particular county.

PRIMARY DOCUMENTS

A primary document is something created by an eyewitness to an event, someone who was there when the event happened. It can be an official document, like a birth certificate, or it can simply be a journal or letter written by an eyewitness. The sooner the document is created after the event, the better.

PROBATE

The court process of distributing a deceased person's wealth and possessions.

SECONDARY DOCUMENT

A document that is usually created after an event, by people who didn't directly witness it. For example, the 1930 census records show how long two people have been married. Since the census may have been created decades after the marriage, it would be considered a secondary document.

SOCIAL HISTORY

The history that explores the daily life of regular people.

Index

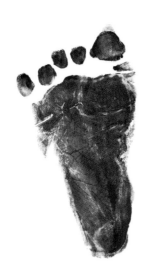
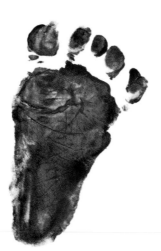